Chains of Justice

Nozick's Entitlement Unraveled

The Curious Philosopher

Copyright Page

Disclaimer

The views and opinions expressed in this book are those of the author(s) and do not necessarily reflect the official policy or position of any other agency, organization, employer, or company. The contents of this book are for informational and educational purposes only and are not intended to serve as professional advice, diagnosis, or treatment.

The information provided in this book is believed to be accurate and reliable as of the date of publication. However, it may include some errors or inaccuracies, and no warranty or guarantee is provided regarding the accuracy, timeliness, or applicability of the content.

Readers are encouraged to consult with professional philosophers, educators, or other qualified professionals where appropriate for personalized advice. The author(s) and publisher shall not be liable for any loss, damage, or harm caused or alleged to be caused, directly or indirectly, by the information or ideas contained, suggested, or referenced in this book.

Chapter 1: Introduction: The Philosophical Landscape

Have you ever walked through a bustling marketplace, marveling at the variety of goods and services, wondering how they got there? Or maybe you've pondered about the sense of fairness – who has the right to what and why? If these questions have ever tickled your brain, then you're in for a treat as we dive deep into the world of philosophical ideas.

A New Dawn: The Rise of Libertarianism

Let's start with a simple scene. Imagine a world where every individual gets to decide for themselves how they want to lead their lives. They get to choose where they work, what they eat, how they spend their money, and even what they believe in, without excessive interference from any overarching authority. Sounds liberating, right?

That's the essence of libertarianism. It's like a bird that believes in spreading its wings and soaring high without any chains. Over the past few decades, this ideology has gained popularity, championing the idea that personal freedom and minimal government intervention are key to a prosperous society.

But, as with everything, there's more to the story. The journey of libertarianism is intertwined with powerful thinkers and their groundbreaking ideas. And one name stands out in this intellectual parade: Robert Nozick.

Meet the Intellectual Giant: Robert Nozick

Now, let's imagine the world of philosophy as a grand museum, filled with statues of thinkers who've shaped our understanding of the world. Among these, Nozick's statue would surely hold a place of pride. But why? What makes him so special?

Robert Nozick, in the latter half of the 20th century, introduced fresh perspectives that made many sit up and take notice. While many philosophers were busy discussing how resources and wealth should be divided among people, Nozick took a different route. He asked a simpler yet profound question: "What are people entitled to?"

Instead of focusing on what's the 'fairest' way to distribute resources, Nozick turned the spotlight on individual rights and what they genuinely deserve, based on their actions, choices, and agreements. This was a game-changer!

His ideas were like a fresh breeze in a room that had been closed for too long. Nozick argued against the idea that there's one universal formula for fairness. Instead, he believed that justice and fairness arise from respecting individual rights and choices.

Setting the Stage

As we progress through this book, you'll encounter stories, analogies, and simple explanations that'll make Nozick's ideas come alive. We'll unravel his groundbreaking 'Entitlement Theory,' which has been both celebrated and critiqued.

But remember, the world of philosophy isn't about deciding who's right or wrong. It's about exploring ideas, questioning assumptions, and embarking on a journey of understanding. So, fasten your seatbelts, dear reader, as we set sail on this exciting voyage through the philosophical landscape shaped by Robert Nozick.

Chapter 2: Ground Zero: Understanding Entitlement Theory

Imagine, for a moment, that you're at a grand feast. The table is laden with delicious dishes, and around it sit people from all walks of life. Some have plates overflowing with food, while others have just a modest portion. You might wonder: how did each person decide what to take? Was it about who came first? Who contributed more ingredients? Or maybe it's about who needs the most nutrition?

These are questions of entitlement, and today, we're about to get to the heart of it.

The Basics: What's Entitlement Theory Anyway?

Picture entitlement theory as a rulebook that explains who gets what and why. Robert Nozick, the mastermind behind this theory, believed that if everyone plays by these rules, the outcome, however unequal, would be just.

So, what are these rules?

The Starting Point: If you acquire something without harming others or stealing from them, it's rightfully yours.

The Exchange: If you want to give away or trade what you have, that's your call. No one can force you.

Making Amends: If someone wrongfully takes something from another, they need to make it right.

Simple, right? It's all about respecting choices and agreements.

Past Deeds vs. Final Picture

Now, let's delve a bit deeper. There are two ways to look at justice in society:

The Historical View: Think of it as a long, winding story. Every event is a chapter, and to understand if the current situation is fair, you'd need to go back and see how it all began. Did everyone play by the rules? Were there any cheats or unfair advantages? Nozick was a fan of this viewpoint.

The End-Result View: Here, you don't worry about the story. You just look at the final picture. Is everyone happy with their share now, regardless of how they got it? Some philosophers believe this is the best way to judge justice.

A Friendly Rivalry: Nozick vs. Rawls

In the philosophical world, debates are the norm. Enter John Rawls, another brilliant mind. While Nozick focused on the journey (the historical view), Rawls was more concerned with the destination (the end-result).

Rawls imagined a scenario where people designed society's rules without knowing their place in it. Would they make it fair for everyone, not knowing if they'd be rich or poor, strong or weak? Rawls believed they would, ensuring that even the least advantaged got a good deal.

Nozick, on the other hand, felt that as long as everyone got what they did by playing fair, the outcome was just, even if it seemed uneven.

A Thought to Ponder

So, back to our grand feast. Would you be content knowing that everyone got their share by following the rules, even if some had more? Or would you want to ensure that everyone had enough, regardless of how the portions came to be?

These aren't easy questions, but they're central to understanding the fascinating world of entitlement and justice.

As we move forward, remember that in philosophy, the journey is as enriching as the destination. The joy is in pondering, questioning, and exploring these intriguing ideas, regardless of where you stand.

The aim of this chapter is to introduce readers to the core ideas of the entitlement theory, setting the stage for deeper dives in the chapters that follow.

Chapter 3: The Cornerstones: Nozick's Three Provisions

Imagine for a moment that life is a grand game of Monopoly. Each player begins with some money, and as the dice roll, they buy properties, make trades, and sometimes even land in jail. The way they move, the choices they make, and the deals they strike determine the winner. But is the game fair? Are all deals just?

Enter Robert Nozick with his rulebook, which he calls the Entitlement Theory. Let's dive into its three cornerstone rules that help keep the game in balance.

1. Starting on the Right Foot: Justice in Acquisition

Think back to the Monopoly game. Remember how every player starts with some money? That's their initial acquisition. In life, it's about how one initially gets hold of something.

For Nozick, this is the first step to ensure fairness. It's simple: if you find something that nobody owns (like an empty plot in the game) and you mix your labor with it (maybe by building a house or planting a tree), it's rightfully yours. It's like claiming a vacant property in Monopoly.

This idea traces back to our ancestors who cultivated barren lands and turned them into farms. They put in the effort, and hence, they had the right to the produce.

2. The Art of the Deal: Justice in Transfer

As the Monopoly game progresses, players make deals, trade properties, and even sometimes sell a "Get Out of Jail" card. As long as both parties agree without being tricked or forced, the deal is fair, right?

That's what Nozick believed. If you willingly trade something you own with someone else, that exchange is just. So, if you've got a property that someone else wants, and you strike a deal that both of you agree on, then it's all good in Nozick's book. No sneaky business, no force, just plain old agreement.

3. Oops, Made a Mistake! Rectification of Injustice

But wait, what happens if someone cheats in our Monopoly game? Maybe they sneak a few extra bills from the bank when no one's looking. That's where the third rule comes in.

Nozick knew that mistakes happen. Sometimes, people get things they shouldn't have, maybe by deceit or force. In such cases, they should make it right. This could mean giving back what was taken or compensating the wronged party in some other way.

So, if a player in Monopoly were to cheat and get caught, they'd have to return the stolen money or maybe even pay a fine. That's Nozick's way of balancing the scales of justice.

A Thoughtful Pause

With these three rules, Nozick tried to create a world where everyone played fair, respected each other's rights, and fixed their mistakes. It's not about everyone ending up with the same amount of money or properties, but about everyone having a just and fair shot at the game.

And as we continue our journey, you'll see how these rules play out in real life, far beyond the Monopoly board. Each rule has its tales, challenges, and nuances which we'll explore together. Roll the dice, and let's move forward!

Chapter 4: Digging Deeper: The Foundations of 'First Claim'

Let's transport ourselves to a deserted island, untouched by human hands. You're the first person to set foot on it. As you explore, you come across a beautiful apple tree laden with ripe fruits. Can you just claim the tree and its delicious apples as your own? And if so, on what grounds?

Welcome to the world of "Justice in Acquisition," a cornerstone of Nozick's Entitlement Theory. In this chapter, we're diving deep into how someone can rightfully claim something as their own.

1. The First Claim: Original Appropriation

So, you're on that deserted island. You see the apple tree and decide to pick some apples. By doing so, you've mixed your labor (the act of picking) with a resource (the apples). This idea, known as original appropriation, is based on the moral principle that when you put in the effort to claim something unowned, it becomes yours.

Think of it like being the first to spot a hidden treasure. The act of discovering and claiming it gives you certain rights over it. But where does this moral idea come from?

Well, it's rooted in the belief that your labor is an extension of yourself. By mixing it with something unclaimed, you're infusing a part of yourself into it. And that gives you a rightful claim over the resource.

2. The Boundary: The Lockean Proviso

But wait! Can you claim the entire island because you were the first to arrive? Here's where things get interesting.

Nozick borrowed an idea from the philosopher John Locke, aptly named the Lockean proviso. According to this principle, you can claim something as long as there's "enough and as good" left for others.

So, while you might lay claim to some of the apples, you can't hog the entire tree and deprive others who might come after you. It's a limitation that ensures everyone has a fair chance.

3. Navigating Choppy Waters: Criticisms and Counterarguments

As with all philosophical ideas, there are critiques. Some argue that the very act of claiming a resource denies others their freedom. Why should the mere act of being the first give someone more rights?

Others question the logic of mixing labor. If you build a sandcastle on a beach, do you now own that part of the beach? Where do we draw the line?

Nozick, in response, emphasized the importance of a just starting point. He believed that as long as the initial claim was just and didn't violate the Lockean proviso, subsequent transactions would be just too. For him, the roots mattered most.

As we pull our boats from the shores of our deserted island, we're left with profound questions. How do we balance individual rights with collective needs? Where do we draw boundaries?

While the answers may not be clear-cut, understanding these principles illuminates the path to a just society, one apple at a time.

Chapter 5: Trading Spaces: The Dance of Justice in Transfer

Picture this: Two children on a playground, one with a toy car and the other with a colorful marble. They eye each other's treasures, and after a brief chat, they swap. Both walk away smiling, believing they've struck a fantastic deal. But was this trade fair? And if so, what makes it so?

Welcome to the intriguing realm of "Justice in Transfer". As we continue our journey through Nozick's world, we'll uncover the beauty and challenges of exchange.

1. A Gentle Handshake: The Essence of Voluntary Exchange

At its core, a just transfer, according to Nozick, is a simple concept. If two parties, of their own free will, agree to exchange goods or services, then the transfer is deemed just. It's the philosophical equivalent of two people shaking hands after striking a deal.

It's like our kids on the playground. If they willingly trade their toys without any outside pressures, then they've experienced a just transfer.

2. Uneven Ground: Challenges of Coercion, Misinformation, and Power Imbalances

But let's stir the pot a little. What if one child tricks the other? Or if one child, much older and stronger, intimidates the younger one into trading? This is where the waters of transfer get murky.

Coercion: Just like a forced handshake feels wrong, any trade that comes from pressure or threats isn't truly voluntary. It's akin to someone pushing you into signing a deal you're not comfortable with.

Misinformation: Picture a trader selling a 'magical' stone that's just an ordinary pebble. If one party is deceived, can the trade still be considered fair?

Power Imbalances: Sometimes, the playing field isn't level. Imagine a rich merchant and a desperate farmer. If the merchant offers a meager price for the farmer's produce because he knows the farmer has no other choice, is that just?

3. Fair Play in the Marketplace: Myth or Reality?

Given these challenges, one might wonder: Can a free market, where everyone's out to get the best deal, ever be just?

Nozick would argue that it's possible, but it hinges on the starting point. If everyone begins with a just share (thanks to our earlier discussions on acquisition), and all transfers are made without coercion or deceit, then the outcome, no matter how unequal, is just.

However, critics argue that perfect knowledge and absolute freedom from pressure are utopian ideals. In the real world, with its information gaps and power struggles, can any trade ever be 100% just?

As we close this chapter, imagine a bustling marketplace. Traders shout, customers haggle, and deals are struck every minute. It's a world of choices, opportunities, and challenges. As we navigate through it, the quest for justice remains our guiding star, prompting us to ask tough questions and seek thoughtful answers.

Chapter 6: Healing the Wounds: The Journey of Rectifying Wrongs

Picture a stunning stained-glass window. Each shard, a masterpiece of color and design, coming together to create something breathtaking. But what if one piece was out of place? Or worse, what if a piece was broken? Would it not be our instinct to fix it, to restore the window to its original beauty?

Much like this window, society too is a tapestry of events, decisions, and actions. And sometimes, mistakes happen. But how do we mend these missteps? Enter the realm of "Rectification of Injustice".

1. When Shadows Fall: Assessing Past Injustices

The first step in healing is acknowledging the wound. In societal terms, this means recognizing when injustices have occurred. Maybe it was a group of people being denied their rights, or perhaps a piece of land wrongly taken.

These wrongs, often deep-rooted in history, cast long shadows. And to address them, we must first assess their extent and impact. It's akin to examining our stained-glass window, identifying the broken shards, and understanding how they affect the whole.

2. Walking the Tightrope: Practicality vs. Ideology

With an understanding of the past, we are faced with a challenge: How do we rectify history? It's a delicate balance between what's ideal and what's practical.

On one hand, there's the ideological approach. If a land was taken, it should be returned. If a wrong was done, it must be righted. It's the notion of restoring the original state, like replacing a broken shard in our window with an exact replica.

But then, there's the practical side. Can all stolen lands be returned after centuries? Can every historical wrong be righted in a modern context? Sometimes, it might be about finding the closest approximation, like patching our window with a shard that's similar, if not identical.

3. In Today's World: Reparations, Land Returns, and Beyond

Modern society grapples with these very questions. From discussions about reparations for past atrocities to debates on returning lands to indigenous peoples, the quest for rectification is very much alive.

Reparations: Some argue that compensating descendants of those wronged in the past is a way to mend historical injustices. It's like offering a monetary value for a broken shard, acknowledging its worth and the loss it represents.

Land Returns: Giving back lands, sometimes symbolic and sometimes literal, is another way societies try to heal. It's akin to placing a shard back in its rightful place, restoring a piece of the broken whole.

Yet, with each of these actions come challenges. Who decides the value of reparations? Can all lands ever be returned? The answers aren't straightforward, but the discussions, driven by the desire for justice, are crucial.

As we step back and admire our stained-glass window, with its vibrant colors and intricate patterns, we're reminded of the beauty of a just society. And even if a shard is amiss or a piece not quite right, the effort to mend, to heal, and to rectify, adds a unique beauty of its own.

Chapter 7: The Guardian at the Gate: Nozick's Dream of a Lean State

Imagine living in a town with a single, silent guardian who only comes out at night. Their sole job? To keep watch, ensure no harm befalls the residents, and step in only when there's a threat. No mingling, no influencing, no involvement in the daily lives of the people. This guardian is Nozick's vision of an ideal state, and we call it the "Minimal State."

1. The Quiet Guardian: The Rise of the Night-Watchman State

In our shared history of civilizations, states have donned many hats, from ruler to provider, from warrior to healer. But Nozick envisioned a state stripped down to its most basic role - like our imagined night-guardian, simply watching over its inhabitants.

This night-watchman state, as it's often called, exists solely to protect individual rights. It's not involved in welfare, not in the economy, not in personal choices. It's the epitome of minimalism in governance.

2. The Boundaries of Vigilance: Protection, Enforcement, and State Limits

But what does this guardian do, and more importantly, what does it refrain from doing?

Protection: Just as our guardian would protect the town from external threats, Nozick's minimal state ensures defense against external aggressions. It's the shield defending its people from outside harm.

Enforcement: If there's a dispute between residents in our town, our guardian steps in to resolve it. Similarly, the minimal state provides a justice system to enforce contracts and settle disagreements.

However, the crucial element is what this state doesn't do. It doesn't redistribute wealth, it doesn't provide healthcare or education, and it doesn't meddle in personal choices. Its power is limited, its reach restricted, its role defined.

3. Voices from the Town Square: Critiques of the Minimal State

But as the dawn breaks, and our guardian retreats, murmurs arise in the town square. Is such a hands-off approach truly feasible? Is it desirable?

Critics argue that the minimal state, in its quest for minimalism, might neglect the vulnerable. Without welfare, without support systems, what happens to those who fall behind?

There's also the debate on feasibility. In a complex, interconnected world, can a state truly restrict itself to such basic functions? And if it can, should it?

While Nozick championed the beauty of individual freedom and limited interference, the critiques present compelling concerns about the real-world implications of such a vision.

As the sun sets again, our guardian prepares for another night's watch, and we're left pondering. What do we seek in a state? A silent guardian, a proactive leader, or something in between? The answers aren't straightforward, but the journey to find them is a quest worth undertaking.

Chapter 8: In the Court of Ideas: Debating Nozick's Vision

Picture a grand hall filled with passionate orators, each stepping onto a pedestal to voice their thoughts, critique, and admiration. In the center stands a statue of Nozick, silent yet evoking fervent reactions from all corners. Today, we join this animated debate on the floor, diving deep into contemporary discussions about Nozick's ideas.

1. The Scales of Justice: Equality vs. Entitlement

At one end of the hall, a speaker argues fervently about the beauty of equality, where every individual, regardless of background, has equal access to life's gifts. They dream of a world where the starting line is the same for everyone, ensuring fairness.

Contrastingly, from the other end, echoes the voice of entitlement. Here, the focus isn't on ensuring everyone has the same, but rather that everyone gets what they deserve based on their actions and choices. It's not about where you start, but how you play the game.

This debate between equality and entitlement is age-old, yet remains as fresh as ever. Which scale of justice weighs heavier? Is it more important to ensure equal outcomes or to honor individual rights and merits?

2. Heart vs. Mind: Is the Entitlement Theory Too Cold-Hearted?

A hush descends as a new speaker takes the stage. They paint a picture of a child born in adversity, asking, "Does the entitlement theory, in all its logical glory, forget the beating heart of humanity?"

The criticism is clear: Some argue that Nozick's framework, while intellectually sound, might lack compassion. By focusing strictly on entitlement and just acquisitions, does it turn a blind eye to those less fortunate? Is there room for empathy, for helping those left behind in this race of life?

3. The Shield Bearers: Nozick's Defenders

As the murmurs grow, a group steps forward, the defenders of Nozick's vision. They argue that many criticisms arise from misunderstandings.

Nozick's theory doesn't oppose charity or goodwill. It merely states that such actions should be voluntary, not enforced.

The entitlement theory respects individual choices. If someone chooses to help another, it's a beautiful act of humanity, but it should stem from the heart, not obligation.

Lastly, Nozick's defenders emphasize that his vision is about honoring individual rights and freedoms. It's not about promoting indifference but celebrating autonomy and choice.

As the sun sets and the hall empties, the statue of Nozick remains, a silent observer of the vibrant discussions. The debates continue, the questions remain, but one thing is clear: In the ever-evolving world of ideas, Nozick's vision has carved a niche of its own, prompting all to think, reflect, and engage.

Chapter 9: Titans of Thought: The Nozick-Rawls Duel

Imagine a grand arena, where two intellectual gladiators step forth, armed not with swords or shields, but with ideas and philosophies. The crowd is silent in anticipation as Robert Nozick faces John Rawls. This isn't a fight, but a dance of contrasting visions about society, justice, and the role of the state.

1. The Meeting Ground: Overlapping Consensus vs. Side Constraints

As the dance begins, Rawls pirouettes with his idea of the overlapping consensus. He suggests that in a diverse society, with people holding varying beliefs and values, there can be common ground. People with different outlooks might converge on similar principles of justice, not because they share fundamental reasons, but because these principles fit within their diverse moral or philosophical doctrines.

Nozick counters with his concept of side constraints. He believes that there are certain rights individuals possess which should not be infringed upon, regardless of supposed greater societal benefits. For Nozick, it's not about finding a middle ground but ensuring that no one's fundamental rights are compromised.

2. The Heart of the Debate: Distributive Justice

The tempo changes as Rawls introduces his concept of distributive justice. He imagines people behind a "veil of ignorance", unaware of their own socio-economic status or talents. From this position, Rawls believes, people would choose a system where inequalities are permitted only if they benefit the least advantaged. It's about creating patterns that elevate everyone, especially those at the bottom.

Nozick gracefully responds with a different tune. He doesn't prioritize patterns but focuses on processes. For him, justice isn't about the end distribution but how things came to be. Did someone earn their wealth justly? Was there a fair exchange? Nozick champions entitlements and deserts, emphasizing that if things are acquired justly, then any resulting distribution, however unequal, is just.

3. The Final Act: Who Gets It Right?

As the dance reaches its climax, the audience ponders: Who has the more compelling vision?

Some resonate with Rawls' emphasis on fairness and ensuring that society's structure benefits even its most disadvantaged members. They see beauty in the idea of creating a system where everyone, when stripped of their personal circumstances, would agree upon.

Others lean towards Nozick, valuing the emphasis on individual rights, freedom, and just acquisition. They appreciate the respect for personal choices and the autonomy of individuals.

As the arena lights dim and the two philosophers bow, the crowd realizes that it's not about picking a winner. It's about understanding the nuances, celebrating the complexities, and continuing the dance of ideas in our own minds.

Chapter 10: Navigating New Waters: Entitlement in Today's World

Imagine setting sail on the vast ocean of the modern world. As our ship navigates through digital waves, crosses borders of globalization, and witnesses the storms of climate change, we must ask: How does Nozick's compass of entitlement guide us?

1. The Digital Frontier: Claiming Virtual Lands

The digital age has transformed not just how we live but what we value. Think of the last song you streamed or the e-book you read. Unlike physical items, these can be replicated infinitely without loss. So, how do we apply Nozick's ideas of just acquisition and transfer here?

Intellectual property becomes a hot topic. If a creator designs a software, they're entitled to it, right? But what if someone else, thousands of miles away, creates a similar software independently? Who's entitled then? And how do we ensure that artists, writers, and innovators are rewarded fairly in this vast virtual realm?

2. Crossing Boundaries: The Global Marketplace

As our ship drifts into the waters of globalization, we witness an intricate dance of trades, transfers, and transactions. Goods made in one country, sold in another, and profits transferred to yet another.

In this global bazaar, Nozick's principle of justice in transfer takes center stage. When a brand sells products made by underpaid workers, is it a just transfer? If a farmer in one country sells crops at a loss to feed people in another country, is it fair?

The challenges of fairness in this interconnected world are immense. We need to ensure that trades aren't just legal but also ethical, reflecting not just market values but human values.

3. Storms on the Horizon: Climate Justice

Our ship then sails into perhaps the most turbulent waters: Climate change. As we see islands disappearing and forests burning, the questions of resources, entitlements, and rectifications become urgent.

Who's entitled to the earth's resources? If one nation's industries pollute the world, affecting another nation's farmers, how do we rectify? And in a world of limited resources, how do we ensure that they're distributed justly?

Nozick's idea of rectification of injustice shines a light here. It's not just about what we're entitled to, but also how we make amends when things go wrong.

As our ship anchors, gazing at the vast expanse, it becomes clear: The world has evolved, challenges have multiplied, but the quest for justice remains timeless. Nozick's principles, while conceived in a different era, still offer valuable insights, guiding us, challenging us, and making us ponder as we sail through the modern world.

Chapter 11: Setting Sun, Shining Legacy: Nozick's Enduring Echo

Picture a grand tapestry, rich with threads of ideas, debates, and philosophies. In one corner, illuminated by the setting sun, lies the intricate design of Robert Nozick's entitlement theory. As we stand before this artwork, it's time to reflect on its legacy and muse about its place in tomorrow's dawn.

1. Reflections in the Mirror of Today

Our modern world, with its digital landscapes, global interconnections, and pressing climate concerns, might seem galaxies away from the times of Nozick. But, as we've ventured through this book, it becomes clear that the principles of just acquisition, transfer, and rectification aren't relics of the past; they're mirrors reflecting today's challenges.

How do we ensure fairness in a digital economy?

How can global trades be made just, considering not just profits but people?

How do we address and rectify the damages inflicted on our planet?

Nozick's entitlement theory, while conceived in the corridors of academia, resonates on the bustling streets of our contemporary world, offering insights, raising questions, and pushing us to think deeper.

2. Gazing at Tomorrow: The Future of Libertarianism and Entitlement

The whispers of libertarianism, emphasizing individual freedom and minimal state intervention, are growing louder. As societies grapple with the balance between individual rights and collective welfare, Nozick's vision becomes even more relevant.

Will we see a world where the state is just the night-watchman, ensuring only protection and enforcement? Or will Nozick's principles be woven with other philosophies to create a hybrid vision for the future? Only time will tell. But one thing's certain: The discussions on entitlement and libertarianism are far from over.

3. Adapting to New Horizons: The 21st Century Beckons

Like all great ideas, Nozick's entitlement theory isn't a static monument but a living entity, evolving, adapting, and taking new forms. As we sail into the 21st century, the theory will face challenges:

The rise of artificial intelligence and the blurred lines of creation and entitlement.

The global refugee crisis and questions of land, resources, and rights.

The increasing inequality and the clamor for a more egalitarian world.

For Nozick's vision to remain relevant, it must adapt, grow, and perhaps even transform, embracing the new while honoring its core principles.

As the sun sets on our journey through Nozick's world, his legacy doesn't fade into the darkness but shines brightly, guiding, inspiring, and challenging us. For in the dance of ideas, the steps of great thinkers like Nozick forever echo, pushing humanity forward in its eternal quest for justice, freedom, and understanding.

About The Curious Philosopher

Welcome to The Curious Philosopher, your dedicated platform for diving deep into the world of philosophy. We are more than just a YouTube channel or a book publisher. We are a beacon of enlightenment, making complex philosophical concepts accessible and engaging for all.

Our YouTube channel is a rich repository of philosophy made simple. We take the profound and often complex ideas from the world of philosophy and break them down into digestible, easy-to-understand content. From the ancient wisdom of Socrates to the existentialist thoughts of Sartre, we cover a broad spectrum of philosophical schools and thoughts, making philosophy accessible to everyone, regardless of their background or prior knowledge.

As a book publisher, we take the same approach, transforming intricate philosophical theories into comprehensible narratives. Our books are not just collections of words, but vessels of wisdom that make philosophy approachable and relatable. We believe that philosophy should not be confined to academic circles, but should be available to all who seek to understand the world and their place in it.

At The Curious Philosopher, we believe in the power of curiosity and the pursuit of knowledge. We are here to stoke the fires of your curiosity, to guide you on your intellectual journey, and to help you navigate the fascinating world of philosophy.

If you are someone who is not afraid to question, to explore, and to learn, then you are in the right place. Join us on this journey of exploration, as we make philosophy easy to understand, one concept at a time.

Be sure to visit our Youtube channel at:

https://www.curiousphilosopher.com/youtube

You can also visit us on the web at

https://www.curiousphilosopher.com

Welcome to The Curious Philosopher. Stay curious. Stay enlightened.

www.ingramcontent.com/pod-product-compliance
Lightning Source LLC
Chambersburg PA
CBHW060902260726
48661CB00008B/3413